SHORT WALKS
SOUTH DEVON

SALCOMBE, BRIXHAM AND THE COAST

by Holly Scrivener

Challaborough Beach and Burgh Island (Walk 2)

CONTENTS

Using this guide... 4
Route summary table 6
Map key 7
Introduction... 9
  Walking in South Devon 9
  When to visit 10
  Things to see 10
  Where to stay... 11
  Travel 11

The walks

1.	Noss Mayo and The Warren	13
2.	Bigbury-on-Sea	19
3.	Loddiswell	27
4.	Hope Cove and Bolberry Down	31
5.	Bolt Head	37
6.	Mill Bay and Gara Rock	41
7.	East Prawle and Prawle Point	45
8.	Start Point	51
9.	Slapton Ley	57
10.	Dartmouth Castle	61
11.	Galmpton and Greenway	67
12.	Froward Point	73
13.	Brixham and Berry Head	77
14.	Brixham to Paignton	83
15.	Tuckenhay and Cornworthy	89

Useful information.. 95

USING THIS GUIDE

Routes in this book

In this book you will find a selection of easy or moderate walks suitable for almost everyone, including casual walkers and families with children, or for when you only have a short time to fill. The routes have been carefully chosen to allow you to explore the area and its attractions. Most routes are circular or out-and-back, although some linear walks may be included that use public transport to get back to the start. Although there may be some climbs there is no challenging terrain, but do bear in mind that conditions can sometimes be wet or muddy underfoot. A route summary table is included on page 6 to help you choose the right walk.

Clothing and footwear

You won't need any special equipment to enjoy these walks. The weather in Britain can be changeable, so choose clothing suitable for the season and wear or carry a waterproof jacket. For footwear, comfortable walking boots or trainers with a good grip are best. A small rucksack for drinks, snacks and spare clothing is useful. See www.adventuresmart.uk.

Walk descriptions

At the beginning of each walk you'll find all the information you need:

- start/finish location, with a what3words address to help you find it
- parking and transport information, estimated walking time, total distance and climb
- details of public toilets available along the route and where you can get refreshments
- a summary of the key highlights of the walk and what you might see

Timings given are the time to complete the walk at a reasonable walking pace. Allow extra time for extended stops or if walking with children.

The route is described in clear, easy-to-follow directions, with each waypoint marked on an accompanying map extract. It's a good idea to read the whole of the route instructions before setting out, so that you know what to expect.

Maps, GPX files and what3words

Extracts from the OS® 1:25,000 map accompany each route. GPX files for all the walks in this book are available to download at www.cicerone.co.uk/1253/gpx.

What3words is a free smartphone app which identifies every 3m square of the globe with a unique three-word address, e.g. ///destiny.cafe.sonic. For more information see https://what3words.com/products/what3words-app.

USING THIS GUIDE

Walking with children

Even young children can be surprisingly strong walkers, but every family is different and you may need to adapt the timings given in this book to take that into account. Make sure you go at the pace of the slowest member and choose a walk with an exciting objective in mind, such as a cave, river, waterfall or picnic spot. Many of the walks can be shortened to suit – suggestions are included at the end of the route description.

Dogs

Sheep or cattle may be found grazing on a number of these walks. Keep dogs under control at all times so that they don't scare or disturb livestock or wildlife. Cattle, particularly cows with calves, may very occasionally pose a risk to walkers with dogs. If you ever feel threatened by cattle, you should let go of your dog's lead and let it run free.

Enjoying the countryside responsibly

Enjoy the countryside and treat it with respect to protect our natural environments. Stick to footpaths and take your litter home with you. When driving, slow down on rural roads and park considerately, or better still use public transport. For more details check out www.gov.uk/countryside-code.

The Countryside Code

Respect everyone
- be considerate to those living in, working in and enjoying the countryside
- leave gates and property as you find them
- do not block access to gateways or driveways when parking
- be nice, say hello, share the space
- follow local signs and keep to marked paths unless wider access is available

Protect the environment
- take your litter home – leave no trace of your visit
- do not light fires and only have BBQs where signs say you can
- always keep dogs under control and in sight
- dog poo – bag it and bin it – any public waste bin will do
- care for nature – do not cause damage or disturbance

Enjoy the outdoors
- check your route and local conditions
- plan your adventure – know what to expect and what you can do
- enjoy your visit, have fun, make a memory

ROUTE SUMMARY TABLE

WALK NAME	START POINT	TIME	DISTANCE
1. Noss Mayo and The Warren	The Swan Inn, Noss Mayo	2hr 15min	7km (4.3 miles)
2. Bigbury-on-Sea	Bigbury-on-Sea car park	3hr	9.3km (5.8 miles)
3. Loddiswell	Loddiswell church	1hr 30min	5.1km (3.2 miles)
4. Hope Cove and Bolberry Down	Mouthwell Sands, Outer Hope	2hr 15min	7.6km (4.7 miles)
5. Bolt Head	South Sands	1hr 45min	5.2km (3.2 miles)
6. Mill Bay and Gara Rock	Mill Bay car park	1hr 15min	4.4km (2.7 miles)
7. East Prawle and Prawle Point	East Prawle village green	2hr	6.3km (3.9 miles)
8. Start Point	Start Point car park	1hr	3.3km (2.1 miles)
9. Slapton Ley	Slapton Bridge	1hr 15min	4km (2.5 miles)
10. Dartmouth Castle	Little Dartmouth car park	2hr	6.3km (3.9 miles)
11. Galmpton and Greenway	Churston railway station	2hr 15min	7km (4.3 miles)
12. Froward Point	Brownstone car park	1hr 30min	4.5km (2.8 miles)
13. Brixham and Berry Head	Brixham harbour	1hr 45min	6.2km (3.9 miles)
14. Brixham to Paignton	Brixham harbour	2hr 30min	8km (5 miles)
15. Tuckenhay and Cornworthy	The Maltsters Arms, Tuckenhay	1hr 30min	4.8km (3 miles)

ROUTE SUMMARY TABLE

HIGHLIGHTS
Creek views, flat walking, rugged coast
Coastal walking, tidal river, views of Burgh Island
Woodland, river and open countryside
Pretty coastal village, wild views, hill fort
Panoramic creek and estuary views
Harbour views, sandy coves, clifftop path
Remote village and windswept coastal path
Lighthouse, wildlife spotting, bay views, secret beach
Lagoon, wildlife and bird hides
Historic sites, sweeping views
Peaceful village, hills, river and creek views
Historical beacon, disused battery, coves and rugged coast
Fishing harbour, lighthouse, nature reserve
Linear walk, coastal path, beaches, sea ferry
Picturesque creek, wooded valleys

SYMBOLS USED ON ROUTE MAPS

S — Start point

F — Finish point

SF — Start and finish at the same place

4→ — Waypoint

~ — Route line

MAPPING IS SHOWN AT A SCALE OF 1:25,000

0 KM   0.25   0.5
0 miles   0.25

DOWNLOAD THE GPX FILES FOR FREE AT
www.cicerone.co.uk/1253/gpx

Looking towards the Great Mew Stone in Wembury Bay (Walk 1)

INTRODUCTION

The causeway at Noss Mayo at low tide (Walk 1)

South Devon's unspoilt coast and countryside make it the perfect place to relax and unwind or experience adventure. As a National Landscape, and with Dartmoor National Park, two lively cities, miles of stunning coastline and busy market towns like Dartmouth, Salcombe and Totnes, there truly is something for everyone.

In 2007, the English Riviera was awarded Global Geopark status by UNESCO. More than just a popular holiday destination, the landscape's unique geology and marine biodiversity are astonishing, with plenty for visitors to discover. Evidence of ice age Britain can be seen in Torquay's prehistoric caves, Kents Cavern – the only place in Europe that has evidence of three of four human species inhabiting the same area at different points in time. Wildlife cruises, snorkelling and paddleboarding are popular, allowing visitors the opportunity to observe local populations of seals, dolphins, porpoises, seahorses and guillemots, to name just a few species that call this area home.

Walking in South Devon

The walks in this guide are based south of the A38, in the South Hams and Torbay districts of South Devon. Most are circular walks, taking in key features of each area and making the

Looking back along the Kingsbridge Estuary towards Salcombe (Walk 5)

most of well-signed footpaths. Many will follow coastal areas where paths are often more rugged, but still well maintained. The South West Coast Path – the UK's longest national trail – is clearly marked with the acorn symbol and yellow arrows, making it easy to navigate. The region's topography means that many walks will have climbs; however, these climbs are mostly gradual.

The area is rich in maritime culture, wartime history and ecological importance, and has many family-friendly attractions. With over 120km of coastline between Plymouth and Torquay, the area is enormously diverse and no two beaches are the same.

When to visit

Both coast and country have plenty to offer throughout the year. The quieter months of spring provide an excellent opportunity for wildlife spotting along the wild coastline or in nature reserves at Berry Head and Slapton Ley. In summer, you can escape the heat with a cooling sea breeze or enjoy a swim from pristine beaches. The autumn months are a wonderful time of year for walking, with warm tones of woodland and the deep purple and yellow of coastal heather. Winter is colder and wetter, but with appropriate clothing there is still much to enjoy, and plenty of pubs and cafes to warm you along the way.

Things to see

Make the most of your visit by taking time for other local attractions and experiences. If you are interested in the area's history, the castles of Berry Pomeroy and Dartmouth are not to be missed. Consider booking a tour around Brixham's world famous fish market and learning about fishing traditions dating back to the 14th century. Families ought to make the most of the Dartmouth Steam Railway, enjoying an excursion from Kingswear to Paignton. The ever-popular Paignton Zoo is a hit with children, as are the amusements along Paignton Pier, and there are many boat trips and ferries running along the coast and up the Kingsbridge and Dartmouth estuaries.

The picturesque town of Totnes is a hub of independent shops, boutiques and cafes. The nearby Dartington Estate is worth a visit, as is the arty Cider Press Centre where shoppers will find gifts and locally sourced produce.

Where to stay

If you base yourself in the transport hub towns of Newton Abbot, Totnes, Dartmouth or Kingsbridge, most of these walks will be accessible by bus. As a popular holiday destination, there is a wide range of accommodation available to cater to all budgets and tastes, such as hostels, holiday cottages, bed and breakfasts, and a few luxurious hotels in Salcombe and Dartmouth. Camping is particularly popular in the area, with many unique 'glamping' stays also available. And, of course, the area boasts fantastic restaurants and pubs, serving the freshest local ingredients and seafood.

Travel

Most of the walks featured in this guide are based in South Hams. Two of the routes (Walks 13 and 14) are based in Torbay, but the regular foot passenger and vehicle ferry services between Dartmouth and Kingswear make the Torbay routes very accessible from coastal areas of the South Hams.

The area boasts a wide range of public transport methods that can be used to reach walk start points or add another feature to your day. Cruises along the Riviera coast and the Kingsbridge and Dartmouth estuaries are always popular. Combined with the option to enjoy the Paignton and Dartmouth Steam Railway, you can explore the area via a range of public transport routes, with many 'round robin' packages available to suit your itinerary. The Travel Devon website contains a very useful interactive map with bus routes.

A car is not necessary to reach most of the walks in this guide but may be helpful for more remote locations and in cases where public transport is limited.

The bell to call the passenger ferry across from Dittisham (Walk 11)

Views from the Brakehill Plantation

WALK 1
Noss Mayo and The Warren

Start/finish	*The Swan Inn, Noss Mayo*
Locate	*///fortified.quits.defers*
Cafes/pubs	*Pubs in Noss Mayo*
Transport	*Bus 94 from Plymouth and Yealmpton*
Parking	*Noss Mayo tennis court car park (PL8 1EH) or the tidal car park (check tide times). Alternatively, park at Warren car park*
Toilets	*Creek inlet, Noss Mayo*

Time 2hr 15min
Distance 7km (4.3 miles)
Climb 200m

An easy walk on a wide coastal path and along quiet country tracks

This popular walk, known as 'The Drive', begins in the picturesque village of Noss Mayo on the Yealm estuary. It explores the estuary's charm along the wooded riverbank before reaching rugged coast, with wide views across the sea. You then follow the Membland Estate carriageway before turning inland back towards Noss Mayo.

The tidal car park in Noss Mayo

SHORT WALKS SOUTH DEVON

1 From the Swan Inn, continue down the road for a short way. If the tide is out, cross the creek inlet by taking the steps on your right and walking over the causeway. Alternatively, take the fractionally longer route along Creekside Road and turn right past the tidal car park. Continue to follow the level road through **Passage Wood**, taking in glimpses of Newton Ferrers across the estuary. This woodland is home to wildflowers such as primroses and violets, and a popular birdwatching spot for woodpeckers, nuthatches and treecreepers. At the Wide Slip you will see where the small ferry runs across to Warren Point. Follow the road, passing the Kilpatrick steps, to reach a fork in the road by **Ferry Cottage**.

Wide Slip ferry crossing looking towards Warren Point

2 Bear right, continuing through the woods along the public footpath. Rejoin the road, passing **Battery Cottage** and ascend into the woodland of the Brakehill Plantation. Continue straight ahead on the track to reach the headland at **Gara Point**.

3 From Gara Point, continue along the flat track of **The Warren**, enjoying

Warren Cottage

the expansive views, and reach Warren Cottage. Warren Cottage was used as a summerhouse by Lord Revelstoke when he entertained King Edward VII. Follow the coastal path as it curves along the coastline, turning left to head inland towards the Warren car park and the road.

The island seen to the west, off Gara Point, is the Great Mew Stone – 'mew' being an old English word for gull. The area is rich in wildlife: while it is a known haven for seabirds, dolphins and porpoises can sometimes be seen out to sea, as well as seals on the rocks below.

> ⓘ *Cellar Beach near Noss Mayo was once used as a store for fishing equipment, although today it is better known for its wild Pacific oysters.*

Cottages on Creekside Road, returning to the Swan Inn

WALK 1 – NOSS MAYO AND THE WARREN

4 At the road, turn left and then take the first right down a rough track alongside farmland to reach a cottage. Continue straight on the footpath ahead and reach Hannaford Road. Follow the residential road into **Noss Mayo**, passing the tennis courts on your right. At the crossroads, bear left on Hillhead and walk downhill to reach the tidal cark park. Follow Creekside Road back to the Swan Inn.

Revelstoke Drive

Stone wall on Revelstoke Drive

This walk enjoys part of Revelstoke Drive, which was laid by Edward Baring, Lord Revelstoke, in the 1880s to impress visitors to his estate with a dramatic carriage ride. The nine-mile route continues along the cliffs as far as Beacon Hill before turning inland toward Membland where Lord Revelstoke lived. On sharp bends, several walls – some of which can still be seen today – were built to prevent horses and their carriages plunging into the sea.

Grassy track on a section of the Avon Estuary Walk

WALK 2
Bigbury-on-Sea

Time 3hr
Distance 9.3km (5.8 miles)
Climb 280m

The longest route in this guide takes in riverside, rolling countryside and coastal footpaths

Start/finish	Bigbury-on-Sea car park
Locate	///keyboard.gripes.ringside
Cafes/pubs	Pub in Ringmore, cafes in Challaborough and Bigbury-on-Sea
Transport	No public transport
Parking	Bigbury-on-Sea car park (TQ7 4AS)
Toilets	Bigbury-on-Sea car park

A firm favourite in South Devon, Bigbury-on-Sea offers stunning scenery, excellent local food and a curious tidal island famed for its links to Agatha Christie. This lengthy route heads inland from Bigbury-on-Sea, following the River Avon, passing through the villages of Bigbury and Ringmore before heading back to the coast.

Looking towards Bantham Sands – a popular surfing destination

SHORT WALKS SOUTH DEVON

WALK 2 – BIGBURY-ON-SEA

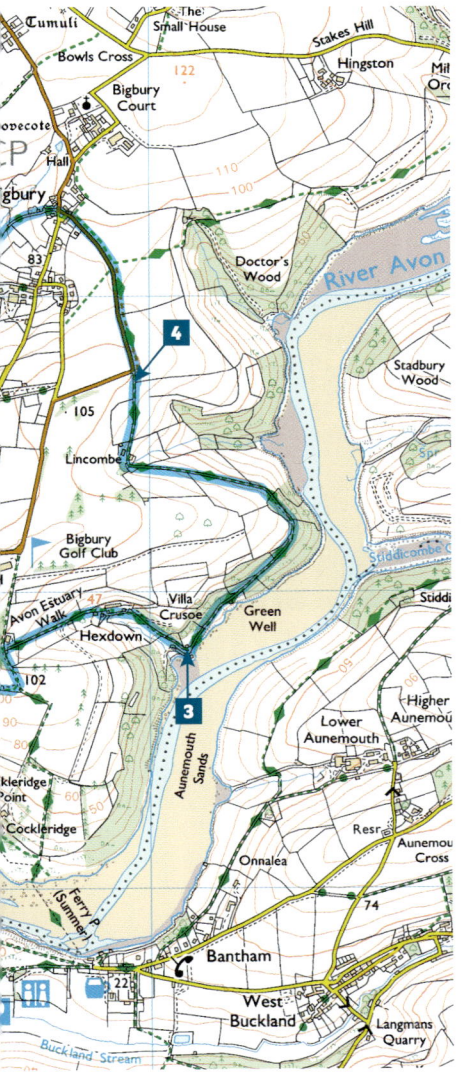

1 Starting at the South West Coast Path (SWCP) marker, situated at the entrance to the car park on Marine Drive, follow the path to the slipway at Sedgewell Cove and continue along the waymarked route to Clematon Hill, enjoying superb views across the River Avon to Bantham. The path leads back to the road. Cross the road and go through the gate into a grass field. Keeping the road on your right, walk uphill through fields until you reach the main road again at **Mount Folly Farm**.

2 Cross the road and walk carefully uphill where you will soon find a footpath to the right. At the end of the field, go through a gate onto the golf course, keeping to the footpath along the hedge line to come to a stone bench. You have reached the highest point on this route at 102m with wonderful views across the River Avon. From the bench, turn left onto the tarmac path through the golf course. At the building, turn right over a cattle grid and down a road, towards the small cluster of buildings at **Hexdown**. Follow footpath signage between the buildings until you reach the wooden gate, then head downhill towards the river to a road.

Looking back at Burgh Island during low tide on Bigbury Beach

3 When you reach the road, turn left uphill, following signage for the Avon Estuary Walk. The single-track road meanders through a peaceful woodland. Continue to follow as it bends right at **Lincombe**. Shortly before reaching the B3392, look out for a small path between two hedges which will lead into a large field.

4 Follow the path to **Bigbury**, keeping the church spire directly ahead of you. Walk through the village, taking the small road straight ahead between two white cottages. Passing the thatched cottage at the bottom of the track, continue down a grassy footpath. Follow this downhill, over a stile and through the middle of a narrow field. You will have views of rolling hills but the sea soon comes into view again. Continuing downhill, cross another stile onto a woody path and turn right. Follow the footpath until you reach a metal gate, cross the stream and follow it down a farm track. Continue to the end of the track, passing underneath telephone wires, where you will cross the stream again.

> ⓘ Devon has the largest road network in the UK, with around 1300km of road.

5 Head diagonally uphill to the top left corner of the field. At the top, follow the boundary of the field until you reach a house, then take the track to **Ringmore**. At the main road, turn left and exit the village. *Or turn right and follow the main road into the village to find The Journeys End Inn, a popular lunch spot with locals and walkers.* At the bend in the road, go straight ahead down a track, passing the National Trust car park. The track narrows into a footpath which brings you straight to the South West Coast Path at **Black Stone**. Here you will be rewarded with dramatic, panoramic views of Ayrmer Cove on your right, and views of **Burgh Island** to your left.

6 Turn left on the coast path as it heads downhill towards Challaborough Bay Holiday Park. Follow the coastal path signs to navigate through the various restaurants and cafes, taking the footpath uphill out of **Challaborough** on the opposite side of the bay. At the top, the path meets the road, so follow this downhill towards **Bigbury-on-Sea**. The Burgh Island Hotel will soon come into view ahead. Follow the road to reach your starting point.

– To shorten

Instead of crossing the main road at Mount Folly Farm, take the footpath to your left and continue straight, descending the valley and then climbing steeply uphill directly to Ringmore. This will save 3.8km and 1hr.

Burgh Island

It is well worth planning your visit in advance to incorporate a loop of Burgh Island, perhaps including a stop at the Pilchard Inn. Depending on the tide, you could walk across the sand bar or take the sea tractor to the island. Climb to the top of Burgh Island for 360-degree views. If you have time, do not miss out on afternoon tea at the Burgh Island Hotel, enjoying its 1920s Art Deco interior. Agatha Christie's novels *And Then There Were None* and *Evil Under the Sun* were both set on Burgh Island – Christie was inspired by the island and retreated there to write on many occasions.

A gentle descent with views of Burgh Island

WALK 2 – BIGBURY-ON-SEA

Loddiswell church

WALK 3
Loddiswell

Start/finish	Loddiswell church
Locate	///simply.steams.denim
Cafes/pubs	Pub in Loddiswell and cafe at Avon Mill Garden Centre
Transport	Bus 162 from Kingsbridge
Parking	Loddiswell car park (TQ7 4QH) or Avon Mill Garden Centre
Toilets	Loddiswell car park

Time 1hr 30min
Distance 5.1km (3.2 miles)
Climb 150m

Visit the sleepy Devon village of Loddiswell and follow woody trails through the Avon valley

This circular walk from the village leads out into the surrounding countryside on a mix of narrow lanes and footpaths. It meanders along the River Avon, along the disused railway track and past the old Loddiswell railway station. The return to Loddiswell village passes the Avon Mill Garden Centre, which makes a good rest stop, or a good alternative starting point should you wish to avoid the steep climb back into Loddiswell.

Fields of wildflowers

Clear waters of the River Avon

1 Take the narrow tarmac road to the left of the church entrance, between the two graveyards. Follow the road as it leaves the village, continuing straight at the crossroads signposted towards **Reads Farm**. The quiet road continues gradually downhill until it reaches the farm.

2 Take the signposted public footpath to your right. Follow the footpath as it skirts the field boundary and enters a small woodland. Cross the footbridge and the path emerges onto a grassy slope. Follow the path back into woodland where it will meet the **River Avon**. From here, continue to walk with the river on your right. The path is easy to follow, but there are areas where fallen trees will need to be navigated around. At the end of this 1km stretch, climb a few steps to reach the old railway bridge.

The 'Primrose' Railway Line operated between Kingsbridge and South Brent from 1893 to 1963. Lack of use led to the line's closure, despite much local opposition. It is aptly named given the

WALK 3 – LODDISWELL

abundance of spring primroses to be found along its route.

3 Turn right onto the bridge across the River Avon, descending back down to the footpath on the opposite side. Return through **Woodleigh Wood**, which is alive with bluebells in the spring, and follow the route of the old railway track alongside the river. Towards the end of the path, you will pass the old Loddiswell Station, now used as private accommodation.

> ⓘ *Archaeological discoveries of ancient settlements and burial sites make the area around Loddiswell particularly interesting, and there is a prehistoric hill fort, the Blackdown Rings, just a few miles north of the village.*

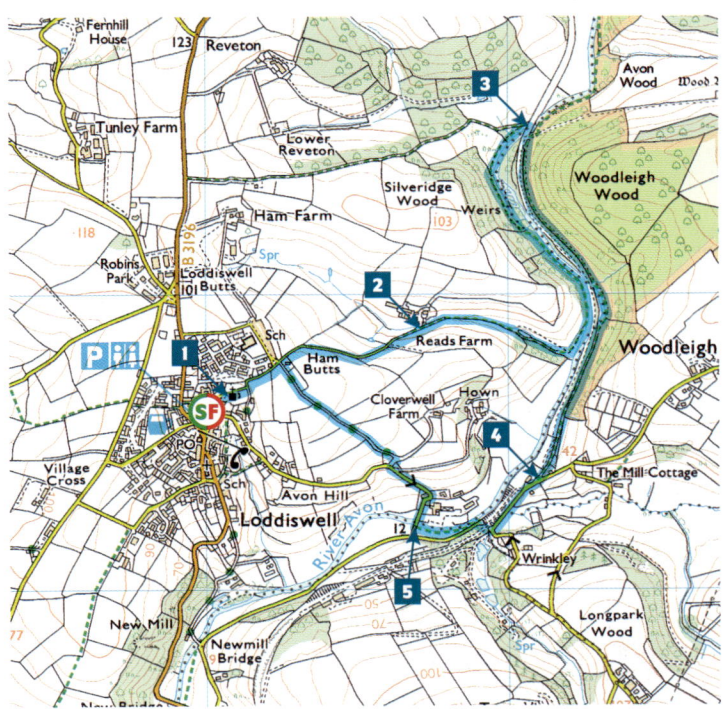

Grassy path heading towards Avon Mill Bridge

4 At the road, walk straight ahead and underneath a tunnel. Shortly after, take a footpath on the right side of the road, through a gate. Follow the grassy path ahead to reach the road at a stile, then turn right over Avon Mill bridge. Here you will arrive at the Avon Mill Garden Centre, an excellent place to stop for refreshments.

Cottages at Avon Mill

5 Continue along the road past a cluster of cottages at Avon Mill. The road climbs steeply straight ahead. At the top, take the second right indicated as Cloverwell Farm, then take the immediate left turn onto a narrow track between hedges. At the end of the track, you will return to the crossroads. Turn left, following the road back to the church.

WALK 4
Hope Cove and Bolberry Down

Start/finish	Mouthwell Sands, Outer Hope
Locate	///germinate.myths.alpha
Cafes/pubs	Plenty of choice in Hope Cove, cafe at Bolberry Down
Transport	Bus 162 from Kingsbridge
Parking	Outer Hope (TQ7 3HG) or Inner Hope
Toilets	Hope Cove harbour

Time 2hr 15min
Distance 7.6km (4.7 miles)
Climb 235m

An enjoyable walk with moderate climbs, extensive views and popular beaches

This route begins in the attractive village of Hope Cove, popular with holidaymakers, before circling Bolt Tail headland and its Iron Age hill fort. Following the coast, the wide path gradually inclines to Bolberry Down, then turns inland down a country lane to reach Bolberry. A gentle climb out of the village takes walkers to a straight footpath with superb views, finally returning to the restaurants and pubs at Inner Hope.

Views across Bolt Tail and Hope Cove

SHORT WALKS SOUTH DEVON

1 From Mouthwell Sands, follow the narrow road past the Hope and Anchor pub towards the beach at Inner Hope. Continue along the road until it becomes a path at the Lobster Pod Bistro. Follow the footpath to reach the road close to St Clements Church, then continue downhill on the road towards the slipway at the far end of the beach. Here, climb the steps onto the wooded footpath and follow onto the headland. Bear right on the path, crossing the rampart to reach the edge of **Bolt Tail**.

2 After enjoying the view, continue along the path, skirting the edge of the hill fort and rejoining the South West Coast Path at the rampart. The route climbs gradually to reach a field boundary. Continue straight, ignoring the path on the left that returns to Hope Cove. Follow the relatively level path over the coastal grassland of

The wide track along Bolberry Down

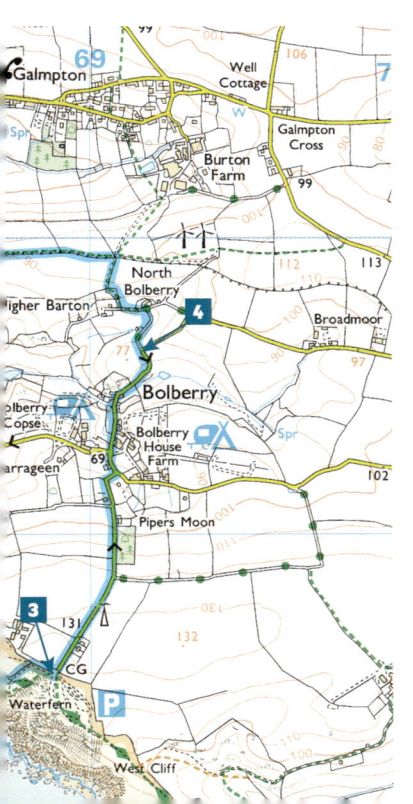

Bolberry Down, home to a variety of wildlife, to reach the National Trust car park. In the springtime, Bolberry Down is a good place to spot Dartford warblers or rare cirl buntings.

3 From the car park, cross the cattle grid, taking the lane inland which descends to **Bolberry**. At the end of the road, turn left and then take the first right down a narrow road. Pass the farm buildings on the right and continue, passing a collection of cottages further down the road. The road

> ⓘ *The Devon flag features three colours that represent its landscape – green for the rolling hills, black for the two moors of Dartmoor and Exmoor, and white for the salt spray of its two coastlines and china clay industry.*

Sunny Hope Cove

narrows and climbs gradually, before a steep incline. At the top of this climb, where the road bends right, take the pathway straight ahead, signposted as an unmetalled road.

4 After a short distance the footpath emerges at **North Bolberry**. Turn left towards Higher Barton Farm, then take the signposted footpath to the right of the farm's entrance. Climb briefly to the top of the field where the path levels. Keeping the field boundary to your left, take the long straight path ahead towards Inner Cove. From here you will see the small hamlet of Galmpton, nestled below, and views

Colourful kayaks at Hope Cove

of Burgh Island out to sea. Follow the path through the camping field, keeping left, and continue straight down the lane to reach the main road. Cross the road and take the footpath directly ahead, which passes St Clements Church. At the bottom of the path, turn right onto the South West Coast Path, returning to your start point.

Bolt Tail Iron Age hill fort

Bolt Tail and the remains of the Iron Age rampart

This promontory Iron Age hill fort was defended by a single rampart running across the headland, making use of the natural defences provided by the steep surrounding cliffs. The site has not been archaeologically excavated, but comparisons with other sites of the age would suggest that the settlement may have contained wattle-and-daub roundhouses, granaries and workshops. From the highest point, dramatic views can be seen in all directions.

The viewpoint at Sharp Tor

WALK 5
Bolt Head

Start/finish	*South Sands*
Locate	*///hours.gently.headings*
Cafes/pubs	*South Sands and kiosk at Overbeck's Garden*
Transport	*South Sands ferry from Whitestrand in centre of Salcombe (summer only)*
Parking	*Overbeck's Garden National Trust car park (TQ8 8LW)*
Toilets	*Cliff Road, South Sands*

Time 1hr 45min
Distance 5.3km (3.2 miles)
Climb 270m

A challenging route with panoramic views of the estuary and English Channel

This beautiful walk takes in the best of the Kingsbridge estuary. With limited parking available around South Sands, the most enjoyable way to reach your start point is via the South Sands ferry from Salcombe, disembarking at South Sands on the famous 'sea tractor'. The route has some challenging and steep sections, but the views from Bolt Head and Sharp Tor are well worth the effort.

South Sands tractor ferry

SHORT WALKS SOUTH DEVON

The rugged cliff path at The Rags

1 From South Sands, follow the road past the South Sands Hotel as it heads steeply uphill towards Overbeck's Garden. Keep left, taking the South West Coast Path ahead through Tor Woods. The path opens onto the coast, following a relatively flat and straight route before climbing up stone steps skirting around **The Rags**, the rugged cliffs beneath Sharp Tor. Here you will have fantastic views of Starehole Bay. Follow the path downhill to the signpost at **Starehole Cove**.

2 Continue to follow the line of the coast uphill towards **Bolt Head**. Once you reach the top, you will have excellent views of Starehole Bay below and Prawle Point to the east. Follow the footpath around the headland and

Views over the remote Starehole Bay

WALK 5 – BOLT HEAD

take the steep climb to reach the signpost and field boundary.

3 Here head inland along the field boundary before heading downhill and crossing a footbridge at **Starehole Bottom**. Climb up again, keeping right where the path splits, and stay on the flat wide track to reach the popular viewpoint at **Sharp Tor**, with superb 360-degree views over the Kingsbridge estuary and Prawle Point in the east.

SHORT WALKS SOUTH DEVON

The path emerging at the entrance to Overbeck's Garden

4 Leave the viewpoint, continuing towards Salcombe. At the end of the path, bear right and follow the path as it bypasses Overbeck's Garden and reaches the road. There is a kiosk at the entrance to Overbeck's, serving light refreshments.

Overbeck's is an early 20th-century subtropical paradise garden where exotic and rare plants have flourished under careful cultivation in this maritime microclimate. It is well worth a visit but note that the garden is closed during the winter months.

5 Take care following the road as this section is often used as overflow parking. The road winds through the woods before reaching the coast again. Continue downhill, returning to **South Sands**.

— To shorten
The walk can be shortened by bypassing the steep climb to Bolt Head and subsequent descent. At Starehole Cove (Waypoint 2), head inland on the footpath along Starehole Bottom, towards East Soar. Reach the footbridge, cross and continue on the route to Sharp Tor. This will save 20min and around 400m of walking.

South Sands in summer

WALK 6
Mill Bay and Gara Rock

Start/finish	Mill Bay car park
Locate	///hoaxes.opened.responds
Cafes/pubs	Hotel at Gara Rock
Transport	Bus CV from Kingsbridge to East Portlemouth (must be pre-booked), or bus 164 to Salcombe followed by short ferry crossing to East Portlemouth
Parking	Mill Bay National Trust car park (TQ8 8PU), or park at Gara Rock near Waypoint 3
Toilets	Mill Bay car park

Time 1hr 15min
Distance 4.4km (2.7 miles)
Climb 175m

An easy walk taking in golden beaches, dramatic coastline and woodland

This beautiful walk is best enjoyed in the spring and autumn months when the popular Mill Bay has fewer visitors. In peak season, avoid traffic and limited parking by taking the short ferry crossing from Salcombe to East Portlemouth and then walking for 20min along the narrow road (or along the beach if the tide is low) to Mill Bay. The walk itself is straightforward, following the spectacular coastal path to Gara Rock before heading inland through peaceful woodland to return to Mill Bay.

Views of Salcombe from Mill Bay

1 From the car park at Mill Bay, take the footpath beside the information board and head uphill through woodland. The short climb soon flattens out. Views of Mill Bay and Salcombe harbour, across the estuary, are visible between the trees. Follow the path and take care to turn left at the signpost indicating the coast path, instead of continuing straight into Sunny Cove. The path soon exits the trees onto **Rickham Common**, with fantastic views of Bolt Head on the other side of The Bar. After 500m, you will reach the lifeboat memorial.

This memorial commemorates the Salcombe Lifeboat Disaster of 1916 in which the RNLI lifeboat *William and Emma* capsized while responding to a wreck near Prawle Point, resulting in the devastating loss of 13 of the 15-man crew.

WALK 6 – MILL BAY AND GARA ROCK

2 From the lifeboat memorial, take the lower path to continue along the coast. The route is easy to navigate, following the path as it skirts above the rocks and hidden coves below **Portlemouth Down**. The maritime grassland here is home to a range of insects and butterflies and is carefully managed by tenant farmers to preserve the environment. When Seacombe Sands come into view near **Rudder Cove**, take the path signposted uphill to your left, towards the white cylindrical disused coastguard hut at Gara Rock.

Memorial to the Salcombe Lifeboat Disaster

Looking ahead to Seacombe Sands beach

43

Coastguard lookout hut at Gara Rock

The coastguard lookout at Gara Rock offers superb views out to sea. It would have been used in the 19th century to detect illegal smuggling taking place along the remote coast below.

> ⓘ *In the 19th century, Salcombe thrived on boatbuilding, fishing and trade; today local businesses rely on the strength of the tourism industry.*

3 Follow the footpath between the lookout and hotel, then keep left along the gravel track taking you into the visitor's car park. Take the narrow footpath on the left, between two fields, signposted to Mill Bay. At the road, take the signposted bridleway ahead and follow it downhill through the woodland back to your start point.

✚ To lengthen

Instead of taking the steep climb up to the coastguard hut, you could continue for 500m further along the South West Coast Path to reach the stunning beach at Seacombe Sands, with its pristine sands and clear waters. From Seacombe Sand, walk directly to the Gara Rock hotel along the higher footpath.

WALK 7
East Prawle and Prawle Point

Start/finish	*East Prawle village green*
Locate	*///enveloped.mergers.toolkit*
Cafes/pubs	*Pub and cafe in East Prawle*
Transport	*No public transport*
Parking	*East Prawle village green (TQ7 2BY)*
Toilets	*East Prawle village green*

Time 2hr
Distance 6.3km (3.9 miles)
Climb 215m

A scenic coastal walk with some steep sections that reward walkers with breathtaking views

This walk explores the quaint village of East Prawle, popular with campers and walkers during the summer season. It visits Prawle Point, the most southerly point in Devon, and heads along the rocky coastline before reaching sea level around Langerstone Point. Enjoy the remoteness of Horseley Cove and then finish your walk with a steep climb back to East Prawle, perhaps enjoying well-deserved refreshments at the quaintly named Pigs Nose Inn.

The formations around Brimpool Rocks make for excellent rockpooling

SHORT WALKS SOUTH DEVON

Enjoy views of Bolt Head from the bridleway

1 From the village green, with the phone box and public toilets to your right, take the narrow road south signed to Prawle Point. Follow the road to where it makes a sharp left bend and then take the public bridleway straight ahead. At the end of the bridleway turn left downhill to reach the South West Coast Path, enjoying views of **Gammon Head** ahead of you.

2 Follow the path as it hugs the coastline, passing **Elender Cove**. This wild area is carefully managed by the National Trust and is now home to the rare cirl bunting, which can be seen throughout the year. Continue

WALK 7 – EAST PRAWLE AND PRAWLE POINT

along the path, reaching the lookout station and visitor centre at **Prawle Point**.

3 Follow the coast path towards a gate in the corner of the field, passing through and heading downhill. Pass cottages on your left and go through another gate at the bottom of the field. The route is lovely and flat here. Follow the coast path as it hugs the rocks towards **Langerstone Point**, keeping an eye out for wildlife such as grey

> ⓘ *The remote cliffs around Gammon Head and Prawle Point are breeding grounds for cormorants, razorbills, fulmars and little owls.*

seals or even basking sharks, which can occasionally be seen in late spring and early summer. You will soon reach **Horseley Cove**, a popular spot for launching kayaks or fishing.

Coastal path marker at Horseley Cove

WALK 7 – EAST PRAWLE AND PRAWLE POINT

Looking back at Prawle Point and the coastguard lookout station

4 Take the footpath to the left, leaving the coast path, and follow the track. As the track bends, take a footpath on your right which shortcuts up a very steep grassy hill to reach a track at the top. Alternatively, you could continue along the track for a slightly less steep option. At the top, continue as the track becomes a road, gradually climbing and then levelling off to reach the east side of **East Prawle**, returning to the village green.

– To shorten

It may be preferable to bypass the first bridleway section, which is rocky underfoot, by continuing along the road to reach the lookout station at Prawle Point, which would take around 20min and save 1km of walking. From here, continue along the coastal path to Horseley Cove.

Looking back towards the Start Point lighthouse

WALK 8
Start Point

Start/finish	*Start Point car park*
Locate	*///fortnight.splashes.defining*
Cafes/pubs	*None on route*
Transport	*No public transport*
Parking	*Start Point car park (TQ7 2ET) or Lannacombe Beach (limited spaces available)*
Toilets	*Start Point car park*

This popular walk, circling the headland of the Start Point lighthouse, offers plenty of opportunities to stop and enjoy the area. It is an excellent spot to look out for marine wildlife, including grey seals, dolphins, basking sharks and seabirds. The coast path leads to Great Mattiscombe Sand, a sheltered cove, before crossing farmland back to the car park.

Time 1hr
Distance 3.3km (2.1 miles)
Climb 145m

This enjoyable short walk offers expansive views of the bay, opportunities for wildlife spotting and a pristine secluded beach

On a clear day there are abundant opportunities to spot grey seals

SHORT WALKS SOUTH DEVON

South West Coast Path marker showing distances from Minehead to Poole

1 From the car park there are views across the 24km stretch of Start Bay, between Start Point and Warren Point in the distance. From the information board, which shows the location of the lost villages of Strete Undercliff and Hallsands, follow the tarmac lane from the car park straight down towards the lighthouse. About halfway down you will pass a coast path marker, which shows the distance from this point to both ends of the South West Coast Path. Continue until you reach the **Start Point lighthouse**.

On certain days it is possible to take a guided tour to the top of

WALK 8 – START POINT

the working lighthouse, where you can hear about shipwrecks, storms and the working lives of its keepers, as well as viewing the original Fresnel lens.

2 After visiting the lighthouse, head back up the path, turning left at the coast path marker.

3 Follow the rocky coastal route, known as **The Benches**, as it briefly ascends the headland and drops steeply down the other side. Continue along the path which skirts the land and sea, taking care of boulders. In summer this section is alive with ferns, large purple foxglove and wildflowers. Keep an eye out for grey seals

A delightfully wild section of coastal path along The Benches

as you pass Great Sleaden Rock and continue around the headland along the coastal path until you reach the stunning **Great Mattiscombe Sand**, a quiet beach only accessible on foot.

4 From here, head inland along the valley path signposted to the car park. This track gradually inclines parallel to a small stream, through farmland. Continue straight until the path levels out and you reach a gate to the car park on your left.

> ### + To lengthen
>
> **If you wish to explore more of the coast, there are two extension options, both of which add 3.2km (1hr) to the walk. Continue along the coast path from Great Mattiscombe Sand to unspoilt Lannacombe Beach, where you can leave the crowds behind. Alternatively, from the car park, you could head along the coastal path and descend into the quiet village of Hallsands.**

The idyllic Great Mattiscombe Sand

The Lost Village

The Lost Village of Hallsands can be seen from the viewpoint in the Start Point car park but is not accessible to visit on foot. Once a thriving fishing village, in January 1917 dozens of homes succumbed to a violent storm and were swept into the sea. The tragedy is attributed to the widespread dredging of shingle from the seabed, which lowered the level of the beach, leaving the village susceptible to coastal erosion. Remarkably, no lives were lost, but livelihoods suffered and many villagers moved away from the area. Two remaining buildings can be seen standing relatively intact amongst the ruins, although the best view would be by boat.

The pretty village of Slapton

WALK 9
Slapton Ley

Start/finish	*Slapton Bridge*
Locate	*///suffix.blush.launch*
Cafes/pubs	*Pub and village shop in Slapton*
Transport	*Bus 93 Kingsbridge–Dartmouth stops at Slapton Bridge*
Parking	*Memorial car park (TQ7 2TQ)*
Toilets	*No public toilets on route*

Time 1hr 15min
Distance 4km (2.5 miles)
Climb 70m

A straightforward walk taking in a serene freshwater lagoon and the attractive village of Slapton

This walk begins by skirting the edge of Slapton Ley freshwater lagoon, with a number of viewing platforms for birdwatching. The path is generally well maintained although it can become narrow and slippery in places. Turning inland the route follows the reedbeds, before taking quiet country roads into the peaceful village of Slapton. Do not miss the opportunity to call in to the Slapton Ley Field Centre before heading back to the bridge.

Bus stop adjacent to Slapton Bridge

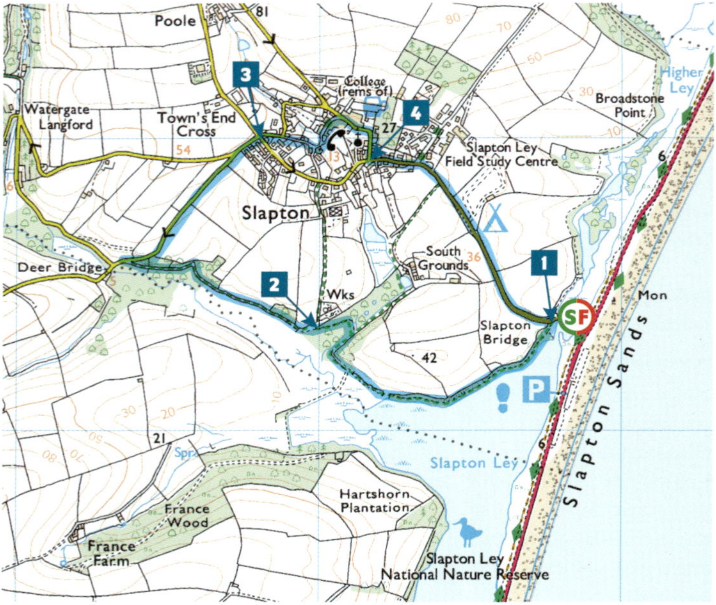

SHORT WALKS SOUTH DEVON

Looking across the Ley towards Torcross

WALK 9 — SLAPTON LEY

The reedbed provides habitat for the elusive otter population

1 At Slapton Bridge, take the footpath on the left, which will immediately open onto a viewing platform and a bird hide containing useful information about the species living in the lagoon. Follow the path ahead as it weaves around the edge of **Slapton Ley**. 'Ley' is a local term for a lake. Pass a pond dipping platform, a large viewing platform and a bird hide which will appear on your left. Shortly after the bird hide, follow the yellow marker as the path turns left and walk along a boardwalk through the wet woodland.

Take time to stop at one of the viewing platforms or hides, offering the opportunity for keen birdwatchers to spot a variety of species from the grey heron to the Great Crested Grebe.

2 At the end of the boardwalk, ignore the option to follow the yellow markers into Slapton. Instead, follow the black markers along a path that skirts the reedbeds and opens onto another large viewing platform. Despite their elusive nature, Slapton Ley remains one of the best places to spot otters, particularly at dawn and dusk when they are most active. Continue straight along the level path, keeping an eye out for wildlife. At the road, turn right and follow as it climbs to the crossroads.

3 At the crossroads, head straight ahead down narrow Brook Street, passing several pretty cottages. Bear left at Meadow Court Barn, continuing on Brook Street as it heads uphill turning right onto Prospect Hill. From here you will have lovely views of the village church and will pass the Tower Inn Pub on your left. Follow the road down into the centre of **Slapton**.

4 Turn left along the main road, taking in the peace of the village. Divert up Wood Lane to visit the Slapton Community Shop, an excellent place to pick up local produce. You will pass the **Slapton Ley Field Centre** on the left.

> The Slapton Ley Field Centre welcomes visitors to its reception, which stocks a range of field guides on the local flora and fauna. It is also possible to book educational nature courses and experiences.

Continue to follow the road back towards **Slapton Bridge**, pass the campsite and enjoy vast views of Slapton Sands across rolling fields.

— To shorten
Follow one of the two alternative routes indicated with red or yellow markers through the nature reserve. These turn into Slapton earlier, avoiding a large amount of walking on roads and saving around 1.5km (30min).

Exercise Tiger Memorial, Torcross

In the Torcross village car park at the other end of Slapton Ley stands a restored American Sherman tank, raised from the seabed in 1984 after its shocking discovery unravelled a long-held military secret. A doomed D-Day rehearsal – codenamed Exercise Tiger – failed miserably, costing 639 American lives. In April 1944, eight US tank landing ships arrived in Lyme Bay, intent on rehearsing on Slapton Sands for the upcoming Normandy landings. Unaware of enemy activity in the area and without escort from a British Destroyer, they were intercepted by German E-boats, who sank three of the tank landing ships. Survivors were sworn to secrecy and evidence of the event was long buried on the seafloor.

WALK 10
Dartmouth Castle

Time 2hr
Distance 6.3km (3.9 miles)
Climb 290m

A spectacular walk along the coast, offering history and stunning scenery, with some steep sections

Start/finish	Little Dartmouth car park
Locate	///outgoing.resembles.changed
Cafes/pubs	Tea room at Dartmouth Castle
Transport	Ferry (summer only) from Dartmouth to Dartmouth Castle
Parking	Little Dartmouth National Trust car park (TQ6 0JR) or Dartmouth Castle
Toilets	Dartmouth Castle

The walk begins at Little Dartmouth and follows a wide track through farmland before entering mixed woodland, tracing the remains of the Gallants Bower hill fort. The path then descends to Dartmouth Castle and St Petrox church, for those who wish to visit or stop for refreshments. The route circles back along the coast path, passing Sugary Cove and taking on some steep sections of footpath before returning via Warren Point. It is possible to start the route at Dartmouth Castle instead, making use of the summer ferry between the town quay and the castle.

Dartmouth Castle and the mouth of the River Dart seen from the ferry slipway

SHORT WALKS SOUTH DEVON

1 Starting at the National Trust car park, take the narrow road through the middle of the car park, passing through the cottages and farm at **Little Dartmouth**. Continue along the flat wide track. Take in the sweeping views and the Daymark beacon seen across the Dart estuary. Enter a steep

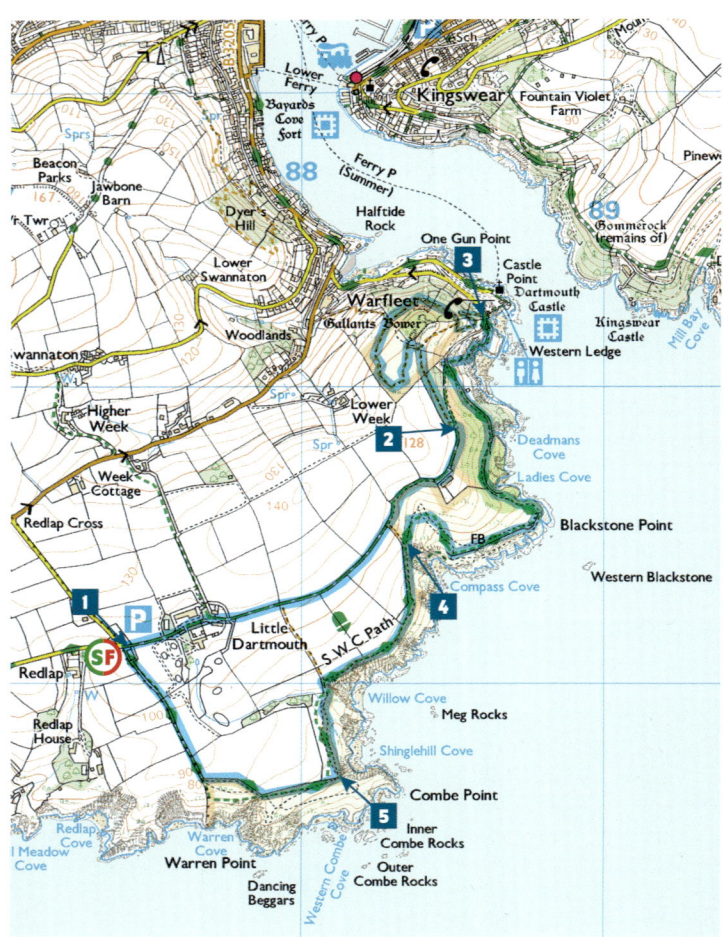

WALK 10 – DARTMOUTH CASTLE

Looking back towards the mouth of the Dart

bending field but keep to the footpath at the top, exiting onto a narrow road by cottages on the other side. Follow the road downhill, keeping an eye out for an ascending woodland footpath on your left, which is not signposted.

2 Keep left and take the footpath as it gradually climbs. Keep left when the path splits, leaving the trees and climbing to the top of the grassy ruins of the **Gallants Bower** hill fort where you will enjoy fantastic views back towards Dartmouth and beyond. Follow the path as it circles the ruins and descends steeply back into the woodland. At the bottom, you will reach a road.

This English Civil War fort was built around 1643–45 to defend against Cromwell's Parliamentarians. On top of the earthen banks would have been a timber palisade. Dartmouth was attacked in 1646 but the defences did not stand up to the assault, and the Royalists quickly surrendered.

SHORT WALKS SOUTH DEVON

3 At the road, either descend the few steps opposite to reach **Dartmouth Castle** (entrance fee applies), St Petrox church and the ferry, or turn right along the road to continue the walk. Immediately take the smaller tarmac route on the left of the road and follow the national trail acorn signs along the coastal path to tranquil and secluded Sugary Cove. Access to Sugary Cove involves descending a series of steep steps from the coastal path. The path then climbs steeply back up the hillside to reach the road again. At Compass Cottage, take the route on the left and follow the coast path through woodland. At **Blackstone Point**, the views open up. Continue to **Compass Cove**, where the path climbs steeply, and keep to the waymarked posts to a path junction. The path on the right heading inland can be used a shortcut, splitting the walk in half.

4 Continue along the coast path, which levels out considerably. At **Willow Cove** you will reach a signpost indicating two routes back to the car park. You can shorten your walk by taking the permissive path inland here, returning to Little Dartmouth. Or continue straight as the path bends down to **Combe Point**.

5 Continue round to **Warren Point**. Follow the South West Coast Path as it climbs gradually inland, straight towards the car park.

In the 19th century, it was common in Devon to designate specific areas for breeding rabbits, primarily for their meat and fur. Place names that include the word 'warren' often reflect where this practice took place.

St Petrox Church

— To shorten

A connecting footpath between the outward route and Compass Cove allows walkers to split the walk in two and complete either the remote Little Dartmouth loop or the steeper Dartmouth Castle half.

Dartmouth Castle

Entrance to Dartmouth Castle

Located at the entrance to the Dart estuary, and situated opposite Kingswear Castle, Dartmouth Castle is not to be missed. Built as early as the 14th century, the artillery fort protected the valuable port of Dartmouth for the next 600 years. The neighbouring medieval church of St Petrox is a fascinating building, but little is known about its origins. Now in the care of English Heritage, the castle is a popular visitor attraction with much for families to explore, including the gun tower, battlements and narrow passageways, as well as a tea room and gift shop.

View from above Greenway, looking upriver

WALK 11
Galmpton and Greenway

Time 2hr 15min
Distance 7km (4.3 miles)
Climb 195m

An enjoyable walk through the charming village of Galmpton, exploring creeks and panoramic vistas

Start/finish	Churston railway station
Locate	///statue.spouse.lure
Cafes/pubs	Pub in Galmpton, pub and cafe in Dittisham
Transport	Bus 12 Newton Abbot–Brixham stops outside golf club
Parking	Brixham Park and Ride (TQ5 0JT, Apr–Oct), or National Trust car park at Greenway (TQ5 0ES, must be pre-booked)
Toilets	Greenway and Dittisham

This walk meanders through the peaceful village of Galmpton, before descending to Galmpton Creek. The route contains a short section of path at Old Mill Farm which is not accessible during high tide, so do check the tide times carefully before setting out. There is an option to extend the walk with a visit to Agatha Christie's house in Greenway or cross the estuary for a stop in Dittisham. Relish fantastic views of the Dart estuary and out to sea before returning to Galmpton along the John Musgrave Heritage Trail.

Marker indicating the tidal footpath at Galmpton Creek

SHORT WALKS SOUTH DEVON

One of the old lime kilns in the area

1 Exit **Churston station** onto the A379 and turn immediately left onto Greenway Road, following the road into **Galmpton**. Pass the pub, village store and church, before exiting the village and turning left onto Kiln Road. About halfway down, pass a restored lime kiln, one of four in the area. At the bottom of the road you will reach the Dolphin Boatyard at **Galmpton Creek**.

2 Follow the road past the boatyard as it becomes a wide track. Keep an eye out for blue plaques for the 'Greenway Walk', which indicate the route to Greenway. The path climbs briefly to Mill Point before descending steeply into **Old Mill Farm**. This is the tidal section of the route, which skirts the edge of the beach before returning inland and a gentle climb up towards the buildings at **Lower Greenway**.

Cross the road, walk straight up through the field and cross a second road into a wooded area. Follow the path through the woodland, emerging into a field, and continue through the field keeping the woodland to your right. At the end of the field you will reach a signpost, overlooking the estuary.

WALK 11 – GALMPTON AND GREENWAY

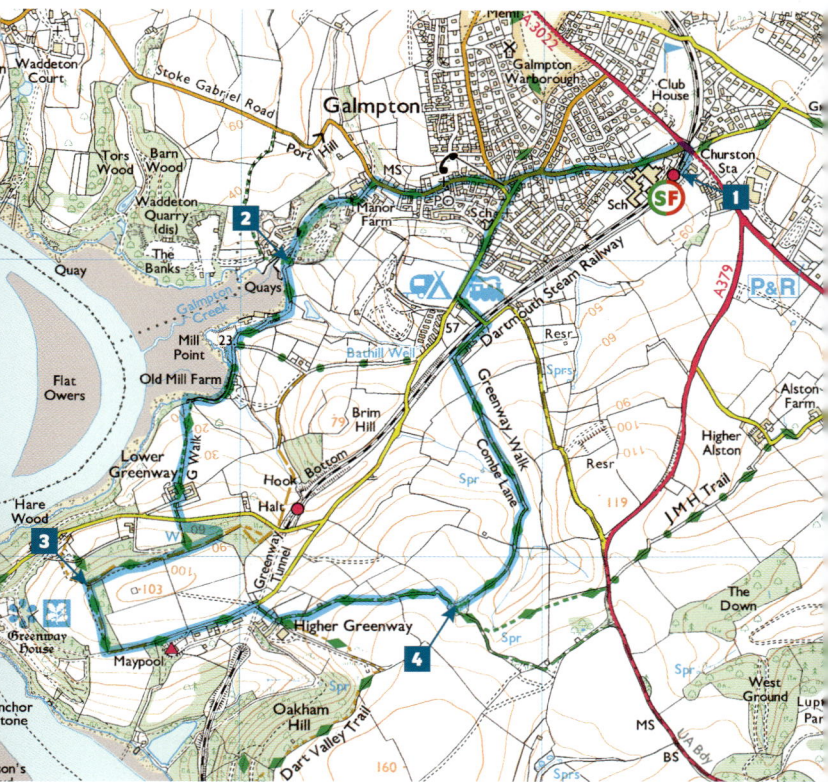

If you wish to visit Agatha Christie's house Greenway, or to take the ferry across to Dittisham, take the path to the right here and descend a steep grassy hill down to a car park. From there, follow the National Trust signposts accordingly.

3 Take the route to the left towards **Maypool**. Pass through a gate where you will see spectacular views of Kingswear and Dartmouth – this is an excellent spot for a picnic break. Continue left onto a country road, then turn right and quickly left onto a bridleway at **Higher Greenway**, signposted to Churston Ferrers. The path climbs

> ⓘ *Queen Victoria once enjoyed a pleasure cruise along the Dart estuary, which she referred to as 'the English Rhine'.*

gradually through fields. When it levels out, a viewpoint offers fantastic views of the Dart estuary to the left and Tor Bay to the right. You will see a memorial plaque to John Musgrave, the former Chairman of the South Devon Ramblers, whom this trail is named after and enjoyed many walks in this area. Continue on the path as it gradually heads downhill to a junction.

4 Turn left at the signpost indicating an alternative route for the Musgrave Trail via Combe Lane. The path descends to cross a railway bridge. If you are lucky, this is an excellent spot to view the trains of the Dartmouth Steam Railway. Turn right at the end of the road, heading back into the village of **Galmpton**. Continue on Greenway Road back to Churston station.

Superb views of Kingswear and Dartmouth

WALK 11 – GALMPTON AND GREENWAY

Greenway Quay

✚ To lengthen

If the ferry is running, it is well worth making the short crossing from Greenway to Dittisham. You don't need to pay entry into Greenway to access the ferry: simply continue in the direction of the house and gardens, following signs for Greenway Quay. To summon the ferry, ring the bell and then enjoy the 5min journey to the quaint village of Dittisham, which has a lovely pub and cafe.

Greenway

This magnificent Georgian house is best known for being the holiday home of Agatha Christie and her family. Born in Torquay, Christie considered Greenway to be a special place, purchasing it herself with the money raised from her books. The boathouse overlooking the Dart estuary featured as the scene of the crime in her Hercule Poirot novel *Dead Man's Folly*. The house – now in the care of the National Trust – and the Christie family have a remarkable history that is certainly worth time spent exploring.

Steep steps down to a searchlight building

WALK 12
Froward Point

Start/finish	*Brownstone car park*
Locate	*///affair.ambitions.velocity*
Cafes/pubs	*None on route*
Transport	*No public transport*
Parking	*Brownstone National Trust car park (TQ6 0EQ)*
Toilets	*No public toilets on route*

Time 1hr 30min
Distance 4.5km (2.8 miles)
Climb 255m

A moderately challenging walk along wild coastline, passing through a wartime gun battery and picturesque coves

This popular circular walk is a firm favourite, offering adventure and history. Crossing arable farmland and passing the Kingswear Daymark, the walk takes you to the site of the Brownstone Battery at Froward Point. The path then climbs dramatic coastline before turning back inland across farmland. The second half of this walk is rugged and a little exposed, which may not be suitable for all. Nearby, Coleton Fishacre and its stunning gardens are worth a visit and could be used as an alternative start point.

Froward Point coastwatch station and visitor centre

SHORT WALKS SOUTH DEVON

1 Exit the car park by following the narrow road south towards **The Tower** (also known as the Kingswear Daymark).

> This Grade 2 listed 80ft beacon, built in 1864, is visible from Dartmouth and from many miles out to sea. It was originally used as a navigational landmark to locate the entrance to Dartmouth harbour.

Continue straight, on a steep descent, until you reach the coast and the coastguard lookout station at **Inner Froward Point**.

2 From the lookout station, head right downhill, following the signs for the South West Coast Path. The path drops steeply and navigates through the trees where you will discover circular gun batteries and the miniature railway of Brownstone Battery.

The Kingswear Daymark

Brownstone Battery was built in 1940 as a defence against the threat of land invasion during World War 2. Manned by up to 300 soldiers, the site consisted of two gun positions, two searchlights, an observation post, cookhouse, soldiers' mess, officers' mess and store rooms.

Location of the second gun at Brownstone Battery

Follow the path down several steps and continue along the rocky coastal path where you will pass the searchlight buildings – from within you can enjoy fantastic views out to sea. Continue on the coast path, which heads steeply uphill until you reach a level open path and signpost.

3 Heading right, follow the acorns indicating the South West Coast Path which briefly stays level before heading downhill and sticking to the edge of the coast. Continue around **Outer Froward Point**, crossing a small footbridge at Old Mill Bay, and hug the coastline along some steep and exposed sections of path to reach a signpost. From here you will have stunning coastal

SHORT WALKS SOUTH DEVON

Looking ahead to Pudcombe Cove

views ahead to Pudcombe Cove, which sits at the base of the Coleton Fishacre gardens.

4 Turn left, following signage for Brownstone car park. Climb steeply uphill, keeping close to the field boundary. You will see the vast grounds of Coleton Fishacre to your right. At **Coleton Barton Farm**, turn left and continue straight to return to the car park.

– To shorten

To avoid the more rugged and exposed sections of the walk, turn left at Waypoint 3, instead of right, heading back towards the lookout station and retracing your steps to the start point. This reduces the walk to 3.8km, which may be more enjoyable for families.

Coleton Fishacre

This National Trust property originally belonged to the D'Oyly Carte family, known for their involvement in the theatrical world. The country retreat boasts an impressive 1920s Art Deco house situated amongst 24 acres of stunning RHS-accredited coastal gardens featuring rare and exotic plants. It is possible to access the South West Coast Path through a gate at the bottom of the grounds, with views of Pudcombe Cove. Visitors can enjoy self-guided tours around the house and gardens, a cafe, plant shop and gift shop.

WALK 13
Brixham and Berry Head

Time 1hr 45min
Distance 6.2km (3.9 miles)
Climb 185m

An easy walk taking in the sights and sounds of Brixham and the beauty of Berry Head nature reserve

Start/finish	*The Golden Hind Museum Ship, Brixham harbour*
Locate	*///awakening.condensed.redouble*
Cafes/pubs	*Plenty of choice in Brixham, cafe at Berry Head*
Transport	*Bus 13 from Torbay Hospital, bus 12 from Newton Abbot, bus 18 from Kingswear. Train to Paignton. Bus 12 or ferry from Paignton to Brixham (Apr–Oct)*
Parking	*Brixham central car park (TQ5 8DY) or Berry Head car park*
Toilets	*Brixham central car park (5min off route) and Berry Head car park*

Berry Head, treasured by the Brixham locals, is a haven for wildlife and a popular walking location. The route begins in Brixham harbour, enjoying the lively heart of the town, before heading out towards the wilds of the headland. A brief climb brings you onto the stunning Berry Head Common where views across Torbay and Sharkham Point stretch for miles. The paths on Berry Head are well maintained and accessible, making it a popular spot for walkers of all abilities.

Extensive views from Berry Head

SHORT WALKS SOUTH DEVON

The Golden Hind replica museum

1 Starting at the Golden Hind Museum Ship in Brixham harbour, keep the sea to your left and follow the harbour wall past various bars and restaurants. Continue through the car park and along the harbour wall, a popular spot for crabbing. Keep to the wall as you continue to Brixham Marina and the **Breakwater Beach**. Keep an eye out for pirate paraphernalia in the area; Brixham is renowned for its annual Pirate Festival which takes place in early May.

2 Cross the pebble beach to the steep steps at the far end, climbing up these to reach the road and turn left. Continue briefly along the road until you see a black South West Coast Path acorn sticker on a lamppost, indicating for you to turn left down a tarmac path. Here you will come across Shoalstone Seawater Pool, a Victorian tidal public pool built into the rock. Continue through the pool, exiting via the car park and turning left onto a road leading up to the **Berry Head Hotel**. Shortly after passing the hotel, take the footpath to your left.

3 Bear left at the top of the steps, which lead uphill through a woodland. Climb gradually until you reach the end of the trees and a wide tarmac path. Follow this onto **Berry Head Common** and through the impressive

WALK 13 – BRIXHAM AND BERRY HEAD

The Breakwater Beach

Napoleonic fort. This is a perfect spot to enjoy a break at the Guardhouse cafe or look out for the nesting colony of guillemots from the bird hide. Continue to the end of **Berry Head** at the lighthouse and enjoy expansive views across Torbay.

> Berry Head was a site of an Iron Age hill fort, which was largely destroyed at the turn of the 19th century, when the area was repurposed and fortified in response to the threat of a French invasion under Napoleon.

4 Retrace your steps and exit the northern fort, taking the path to your left, and follow the coast path for a short distance. Keep left, following the footpath to reach the remains of the southern fort. This site was designed to protect the northern fort from land attack, but it also included the barracks, kitchen and storehouse.

5 Exit the southern fort and turn left, walking to the corner of the Berry Head car park. Take the footpath straight ahead, enter a large field and follow the field boundary. At the edge of the field, turn right onto the track which will lead you back into the woodland. The large octagonal metal structure that you pass is an aid to aircraft navigation. Follow the path and you will soon reach the same path that took you onto the Common. Turn left here and retrace your outward route through the woodland and past the hotel.

6 At the entrance to the Shoalstone Pool car park, the quickest route to return to **Brixham harbour** is by following the road. Be sure to take in the views of the bay to your right and the typical seaside homes along this side of Brixham. Continue along the road until you reach steps down into the harbourside car park and return to the Golden Hind.

Brixham harbour

WALK 13 – BRIXHAM AND BERRY HEAD

Shoalstone tidal swimming pool

– To shorten
Begin at the Berry Head car park, instead of walking from Brixham harbour, and complete the loop around the headland. This gives an easy, flat, circular route approximately 2.4km in length (45min).

Berry Head National Nature Reserve

The Berry Head reserve is part of the English Riviera UNESCO Global Geopark, owing to Torbay's unique natural environment and geology. The reserve features calcareous limestone grassland, rocky cliffs and scrub woodland. It is home to over 200 species of bird, including sparrowhawks, kestrels, kittiwakes, gannets and guillemots. The Artillery Store, one of the old fort buildings, is now home to the greater horseshoe bat which is one of Britain's most endangered mammals.

Beach huts on Broadsands

WALK 14
Brixham to Paignton

Time 2hr 30min
Distance 8km (5 miles)
Climb 250m

Follow the South West Coast Path along the coast, exploring coves, beaches and harbours on this moderately challenging walk

Start	*Brixham harbour*
Finish	*Paignton harbour*
Locate	*///clips.excavate.bothered*
Cafes/pubs	*Cafe at Broadsands Beach and Goodrington Sands, pubs and restaurants in Paignton*
Transport	*Bus 13 service from Torbay Hospital, bus 12 from Newton Abbot, bus 18 from Kingswear. Train to Paignton. Bus 12 or ferry from Paignton to Brixham (Apr–Oct)*
Parking	*Brixham central car park (TQ5 8DY) and Paignton harbour*
Toilets	*Fishcombe Cove, Broadsands Beach, Goodrington Sands, Paignton harbour*

This walk is easy to navigate, yet there are steep and rocky sections that provide challenge. From the bustling fishing town of Brixham, the route explores several remote coves, known for their importance as part of the English Riviera UNESCO Global Geopark, before ascending to clifftops following the tracks of the Dartmouth Steam Railway into the quaint Paignton harbour.

Brixham marina

SHORT WALKS SOUTH DEVON

1 Starting from outside the Rockfish restaurant, situated at the entrance to the working fishing port, take the signposted coastal path in the direction of Fishcombe Cove. Walk away from the harbour alongside the car parks before ascending steps into the woodland of Battery Gardens. Follow the path down into Fishcombe Cove then climb steeply up the tarmac path to the holiday park. Turn right here and continue along the waymarked footpath to **Churston Cove**. Another challenging steep section of steps will take you into dense woodland, where the path becomes relatively level and straight towards **Elberry Cove**.

At Elberry Cove you will see the ruins of an 18th-century bathhouse erected for Lord Churston. The building allowed its patron to swim into the sea with a sense of privacy but, unfortunately, is no longer in use.

2 At Elberry Cove, cross the pebble beach to the far side and continue up the footpath signposted with an acorn and yellow arrow. A climb brings you

Between Fishcombe Cove and Churston Cove

onto the flat fields at **Churston Point**. Keep an eye out for grey seals relaxing on the rocks below. Follow the path, hugging the coast, until you reach the beautiful **Broadsands Beach**, a red-sandy beach popular for paddleboarding, kayaking and swimming. Walk alongside the beach huts to the end of the beach, turning left up a tarmac footpath that takes you underneath the impressive Broadsands railway viaduct to a road.

3 At the road, turn sharply right and go up the steps, bringing you level with the steam railway track. The path stays close to the train tracks for about 1.5km, with several fantastic viewpoints for trainspotters hoping to see a steam train in action alongside the backdrop of Tor Bay, before diverting

SHORT WALKS SOUTH DEVON

Paignton harbour

right underneath the tracks onto **Goodrington Sands**.

4 Walk along the promenade, passing the waterpark and several restaurants, then a small cluster of beach huts. Follow the South West Coast Path markers, which are found as metal discs in the ground, up into Roundham Gardens. This leads back onto **Roundham Head** which you follow until you reach Cliff Road. From here, follow the road down into **Paignton harbour**.

At the North Quay, you will find three kiosks where you can book a passenger ferry return to Brixham. This is an excellent way to finish your walk and you are almost guaranteed to spot Brixham's local seal population resting in the marina.

– To shorten

It is possible to shorten this walk by 4km (1hr 15min), and avoid most of the uphill sections, if you begin at Broadsands Beach, where there is ample parking. Return via bus 12, which stops on Dartmouth Road, a 10min walk from Broadsands Beach.

SHORT WALKS SOUTH DEVON

Dartmouth Steam Railway

The Dartmouth steam engine heading to Paignton

Linking Paignton with Kingswear, the steam railway is not to be missed when visiting Torbay. A trip on the railway can be combined with sea and river ferries around the English Riviera towns of Totnes, Torquay, Paignton, Brixham, Kingswear and Dartmouth, offering visitors an easy round robin experience. The line opened in 1864 and shortly after introduced a branch line from Churston to Brixham, an important fishing town, although this additional line then closed in the 1960s. The Dart Valley Railway company was founded in the 1960s and acquired the Paignton to Kingswear line in 1973 after it was threatened with closure by British Railways. It is now a much-loved feature of the landscape.

WALK 15
Tuckenhay and Cornworthy

Start/finish	The Maltsters Arms, Tuckenhay
Locate	///diverged.serious.tinny
Cafes/pubs	Pub in Tuckenhay and Cornworthy
Transport	Community bus TS from Totnes (Wed and Fri only)
Parking	On-road parking outside the Maltsters Arms (TQ9 7EQ)
Toilets	No public toilets on route

Time 1hr 30min
Distance 4.8km (3 miles)
Climb 150m

An easy walk along the picturesque Bow Creek and through the countryside of the Dart Valley

From the hamlet of Tuckenhay, a meandering footpath keeps close to the water line of Bow Creek through the charms of Bow Wood. There is a small tidal section where the path may become inaccessible during high tide, so it is important to check the tides beforehand. The route then circles into the village of Cornworthy before returning to Tuckenhay via a shaded unmetalled road over Corkscrew Hill.

Rolling countryside at Efford's Close Copse

SHORT WALKS SOUTH DEVON

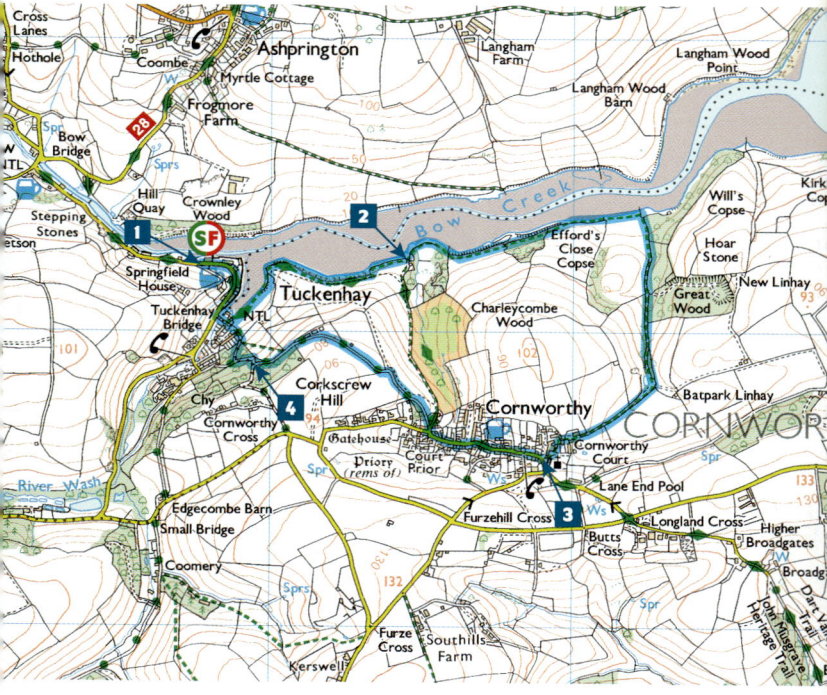

1 From the pub, walk down the road towards **Tuckenhay Bridge**, enjoying picturesque views of Bow Creek between houses. Turn left onto the bridge and, shortly after, take the signposted footpath on the left, crossing a stile. From here the footpath is clearly waymarked and follows the edge of **Bow Creek** through Bow Wood to reach a signpost.

Bow Wood is home to a wide variety of plants and wildlife, including over 13,000 native trees and shrubs, birds such as yellowhammers, buzzards and skylarks, and butterflies.

2 At the signpost, continue straight through the gate at Charlecombe Meadow towards **Efford's Copse Close**. The footpath descends gradually through the woods before turning

Watercraft at Bow Creek

On the shores of Bow Creek

onto the tidal section of beach. Pass through the gate into a field. At the end of the field, turn right uphill, following the edge of the field boundary. At the top of the hill, pass a small pond and bear right along a farm track to reach a working farm. Follow the signage carefully through the farm to reach the road into **Cornworthy**.

3 At the road turn right, passing the local pub, as far as Hothill Lane on your right. A few metres up the lane, take the unmetalled road on the left between the two houses. The path climbs up **Corkscrew Hill** before descending steeply through a wooded area to a fork.

The Maltsters Arms in Tuckenhay

WALK 15 — TUCKENHAY AND CORNWORTHY

> ⓘ *The mill in Tuckenhay once produced paper and the quays were used for unloading goods such as limestone, coal and cider.*

4 Keep right and right again at the second fork. Continue downhill to houses in **Tuckenhay**. Retrace your steps back across the bridge and along the road to the pub.

− To shorten

Turn inland at Waypoint 2 along the footpath to Cornworthy. This is also a good alternative if the tide is too high to continue along Bow Creek. The path rejoins the main route at Hothill Lane.

The peaceful village of Tuckenhay sits along Bow Creek

SHORT WALKS SOUTH DEVON

Clockwise from top: SWCP marker signals your start point (Walk 2); Village church in Slapton (Walk 9); Paignton harbour (Walk 14); Crossing a footbridge (Walk 15)

USEFUL INFORMATION

Tourism bodies

English Riviera
www.englishriviera.co.uk

English Riviera UNESCO Global Geopark
http://englishrivierageopark.org.uk

Torbay Coast and Countryside Trust
www.countryside-trust.org.uk

South Hams
www.southhams.com

Visit South Devon
www.visitsouthdevon.co.uk

Tourist information centres

Dartmouth Visitor Centre, The Quay, tel 01803 834224

English Riviera Visitor Information Centre, Torquay, near harbour, tel 01803 211211

Kingsbridge Information Centre, The Quay, tel 01548 853195

Salcombe Information Centre, Market Street, tel 01548 843927

Travel

Dartmouth Castle Ferry
www.dartmouthcastleferry.co.uk

Dartmouth Steam Railway and River Boat Company
www.dartmouthrailriver.co.uk

Greenway Ferry
www.greenwayferry.co.uk

South Sands Ferry
www.southsandsferry.co.uk

Travel Devon
www.traveldevon.info

Attractions

Burgh Island
www.burghisland.com

Coleton Fishacre, National Trust
www.nationaltrust.org.uk/visit/devon/coleton-fishacre

Dartmouth Castle
www.english-heritage.org.uk/visit/places/dartmouth-castle

Greenway, National Trust
www.nationaltrust.org.uk/visit/devon/greenway

Kents Cavern Prehistoric Caves
www.kents-cavern.co.uk

Overbeck's Garden, National Trust
www.nationaltrust.org.uk/visit/devon/overbecks-garden

Slapton Ley National Nature Reserve
www.field-studies-council.org/locations/slaptonley

Walking information

Countryside Code
www.gov.uk/government/publications/the-countryside-code

South West Coast Path
www.southwestcoastpath.org.uk

© Holly Scrivener 2025
First edition 2025
ISBN: 978 1 78631 253 2
eISBN: 978 1 78765 218 7

Printed in Singapore by KHL Printing using responsibly sourced paper.
A catalogue record for this book is available from the British Library.
All photographs are by the author unless otherwise stated.
Cover illustration of Kingswear and the River Dart by Avery Mitchell.

© Crown copyright and database rights 2025 OS AC0000810376

Cicerone's EU representative for GPSR compliance is Easy Access System Europe, Mustamäe tee 50, 10621 Tallinn, Estonia. Email gpsr.requests@easproject.com.

CICERONE

Cicerone Press, Juniper House, Murley Moss, Oxenholme Road,
Kendal, Cumbria, LA9 7RL

www.cicerone.co.uk

Updates to this Guide

While every effort is made to ensure the accuracy of guidebooks as they go to print, changes can occur during the lifetime of an edition. Any updates that we know of for this guide will be on the Cicerone website (www.cicerone.co.uk/1253/updates), so please check before planning your trip. We also advise that you check information about transport, accommodation and shops locally. Even rights of way can be altered over time. We are always grateful for information about any discrepancies between a guidebook and the facts on the ground, sent by email to updates@cicerone.co.uk.

Register your book: To sign up to receive free updates, special offers and GPX files where available, create a Cicerone account and register your purchase via the 'My Account' tab at www.cicerone.co.uk.